FIRE ISLAND
IN COLOR

by JEFF RICHARDS

CONTENTS

KYX PRESS, P.O BOX 336 SAYVILLE, NEW YORK 11782-0336

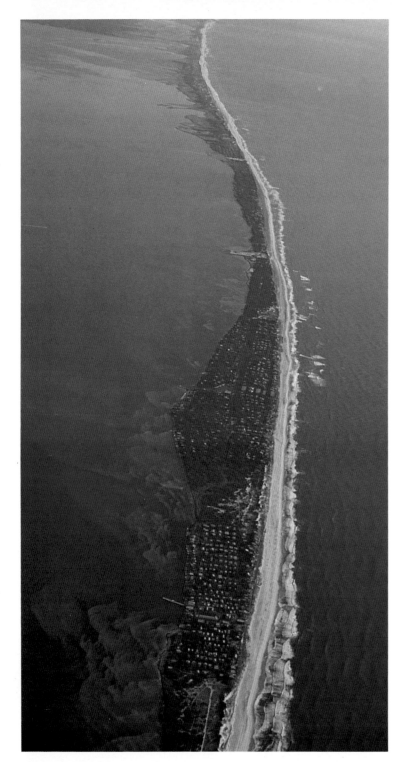

Acknowledgements

I'd most like to thank my parents whose extraordinary help went way beyond familial responsibility. They gave me editorial and moral support; and good-naturedly relinquished their dining room for the many months I needed a workspace. Without them, this book and, of course, this author would not exist.

Then there's Mike Madigan - photographer, Mac maven and Renaissance man of prodigious gifts.I was indeed fortunate to meet him early on as his encyclopedic knowledge, technical expertise and aesthetic excellence fueled this project almost from its inception.

Bill Rudock, of Our View Safaris, photographed the aerials in this book. He is amazing! He has a thriving photo studio, an aerial photography business, plans and leads photo safaris, gives seminars, is a flight instructor and qualified diver, and somehow finds time to work full time for the Suffolk County Police Department. I can only scratch my head in wonderment.

Pete Nawrocky, a Queens-based underwater photographer, graciously shared some of his many exquisite photos with me. His artistry is obvious; his generosity immeasurable.

I'm greatly indebted to the people at the Fire Island National Seashore, not only for giving me the run of their archives, but on a much larger scale, for their dedication, skill and humanity. Their love of their mission is unmistakable. There could be no better stewardship of such a glorious resource.

Many thanks to Ted Lap, Edith and Jeff Willcox, Joanne Rosché, Ken Ruzicka, John Scala, Steve Salinger and Warren Wexler for their invaluable contributions.

Of special note: Warren Mcdowell, publisher of the Fire Island Tide, gave me an editorial assignment that caught me up in this Fire Island experience afresh. For that, and for his unrelenting sense of fun, I am grateful.

In fact, quite as soul-stirring as the splendor of Fire Island has been, has been the opportunity to meet and work with such fascinating, generous and able people. I have been blessed.

Library of Congress Catalog Card Number : 91-090561

ISBN 0-962-8881-0-9 Hardcover
ISBN 0-962-8881-1-7 Softcover

INTRODUCTION

On a clear day, from a high Fire Island rooftop, one can see the Manhattan skyline. Yet in spirit and in substance, Fire Island seems nearer the South Pacific than tumultuous Gotham. Every summer weekend, New York's own huddled masses, yearning to breath free, flock to the docks at Bay Shore, Sayville and Patchogue to cast off for Fire Island's golden shore.

They know what they're doing. With its abundance of resources, it would be hard to imagine a more salutary geographic adjacency. It's no wonder that Fire Island has become, in less than a century, New York's favorite neighborhood resort.

Fire Island is not all that old. Long Island is formed largely of material deposited by glaciers, the last of which receded less than 25,000 years ago. Fire Island surely post-dates "The Big Fish"; though by how long is uncertain. Geologically, its dynamics are impressive. We know that the western end has grown by six miles since 1858 due to the littoral drift, and that the Island is slowly moving landward. We know that there is a continual, seasonal alternation of sand deposition from barrier beach to offshore sandbar. Hurricanes and storms regularly change the face of the Island and wreak havoc with the handiwork of man. There is an ongoing debate as to whether man should be allowed to rebuild the homes that nature will inevitably wash away. Indeed, that is one of the National Seashore's primary concerns. In the late 1950's, Robert Moses presented a plan to "preserve" the Island by bull-dozing communities and by "stabilizing" the dunes with a full-length roadway. Were it not for the impassioned resistance that plan engendered in Fire Islanders and determined environmentalists, there would today be 32 more miles of Jones Beach. And little charm. Placing Fire Island in the custody of the National Park Service was an idea conceived to forestall that fate. Few would dispute that the plan worked spectacularly well.

Physically, Fire Island boasts, within that meager 32-mile length and less than half-mile width, many distinct "life zones," each with its own different life forms.

The ocean beach, or "berm," is undoubtedly most familiar and beloved.

Behind the berm is the sand dune, backbone of the barrier beach. It is formed largely by wind-blown sand captured by objects in its path, primarily beach grass. Often there is a secondary dune, lower than the first and separated from it by a dry, sandy, somewhat protected valley called a swale.

In the lee of the dunes, thickets and woodlands can flourish; Fire Island's most spectacular is Sunken Forest, a marine forest pruned flush with the dune-tops by wind-driven salt spray. Holly and deciduous trees predominate. There are also forests almost entirely of conifers.

Bayward of these are found freshwater ponds, bogs, salt-water marshes and tidal mud flats. The Bay, of course, is a large ecosystem unto itself.

The animals of Fire Island range from the single-celled to the great whales that occasionally wash up on shore. Countless species of every phylum thrive here. Certain fish and shellfish are targets of entire industries. There are turtles and snakes and toads. Mammals include voles, mice, rats, rabbits, squirrels, raccoons, muskrats, foxes and opossums. Whitetail deer have become so common that close encounters with them can be a daily occurrence. At least 200 species of birds have been counted; seagulls and sandpipers, warblers and woodpeckers, herons and egrets, hawks and owls, ducks and swans and on and on. It is said that more than a quarter of the birds found in the entire U.S. show up regularly on Fire Island.

The variety of plants on the Island is even greater. Those who wish to know more about local natural life will find guidebooks to both flora and fauna available at National Seashore Visitor's Centers. There is even a guide to edible plants.

Though Fire Island's human history is rather more recent, it is no less interesting.

Prior to the seventeenth century, it was used principally by pirates and several Long Island Indian tribes, notably the Secatogues and the Unkachaugs, for hunting, fishing, shorewhaling and gathering shells from which to make wampum. There is no evidence that these tribes established residences on the Island. Still, the arrival of the white man, as usual, eventually resulted in their complete disappearance, even as visitors.

The first major white player on the Fire Island stage was Col. William "Tangier" Smith. In 1675, after Charles II regained the throne of England following the death of Oliver Cromwell, he rewarded Smith for his loyalty to the Stuarts during their exile by naming him mayor of Tangier, hence the nickname. When, for military reasons, England abandoned the North African colony, Smith went to New York, where his abilities and friendships allowed him to rise to political prominence.

Eventually he found loopholes in the Nicoll Patent that enabled him to acquire land from local Indians. This land included all of Fire Island and stayed in the Smith family for several generations. After the American Revolution, Henry Tangier Smith sold his portion of the estate, which included all of western Fire Island, to "Twenty Proprietors" communally, who used the land mainly for grazing cattle.

But in the 1850's, an entrepreneur from Babylon named David S.S. Sammis envisioned a resort hotel on Fire Island and began accumulating proprietary property shares. A lawsuit against him, however, led to a court-ordered effort to resolve ownership of the land. Since many of the original proprietors had died and few subsequent transactions had been recorded, this proved difficult. After six years of attempts were made to reach would-be claimants, Fire Island was divided into 78 parcels; one and a half of which went to Sammis. He built his Surf Hotel west of today's Kismet and enjoyed great success. The development of Fire Island as a modern resort area had started in earnest.

In 1868, Archie and Elizabeth Perkinson opened a restaurant on their Cherry Grove farm that, by 1880, had grown into a hotel that attracted P.T. Barnum and Mark Twain.

In the 1880's, the Fire Island Fishing Company built a pier out into the ocean at a site that later became Lonelyville.

Edward Ryder's Water Island White House Hotel, built in 1890 (or earlier), drew guests that included Teddy Roosevelt.

In 1894, the Chatauqua movement (a prominent Protestant educational and cultural organization), established Point O' Woods as a regional center.

1908 saw the founding of populous Ocean Beach by John Wilbur, whose original 1000-lot subdivision sold out in five years.

By 1958, the last of today's residential enclaves, Dunewood, had arisen (a few others, built in the 1960's, were condemned and later removed). The establishment of the National Seashore in 1964 precluded further development except within established communities.

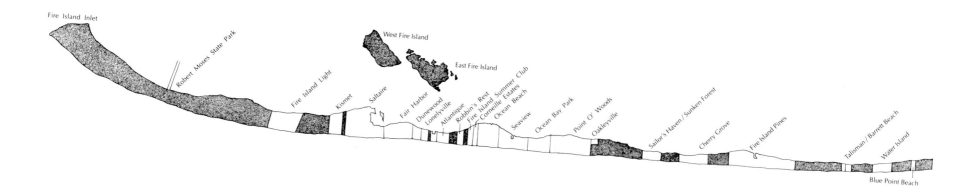

The twenty or so communities that exist today (2 or 3 of them have no more than a dozen houses) differ from each other enormously. There are no roads on Fire Island and, rather intentionally, communication between communities has been limited. Residents tend to be proud of, and a bit proprietary about, their own little parcels of paradise. For example, predominently gay Cherry Grove has a big stake in preserving its status as one of the few places in the world dedicated to that lifestyle. The handful of residents of diminutive Blue Point Beach cherish the privacy its isolation affords just as those of Ocean Beach relish its bustle. The many young singles at Davis Park welcome a place that allows several to share what would otherwise be a prohibitively high summer rental fee. Almost anyone seeking a place in the sun can find one tailor-fitted to his or her own preferences. One of the most delightful diversions Fire Island offers is the opportunity to explore the astonishing diversity of its communities

Because the advent of the Seashore halted the Island's previously unbridled expansion, many feel that it came along at just the right time, aesthetically and economically. Fire Island got to keep its captivating little villages, with their comforts and their tax bases; and more than half of the Island was kept undeveloped; including an 8-mile section designated New York's only National Wilderness. To ice the cake, N.P.S.' superbly designed and maintained interpretive centers at Watch Hill, Sunken Forest, Smith Point and Fire Island Light tell us much about the nature and history of this enchanting isle.

Finally, no introduction to Fire Island would be complete without an allusion to its wealth of entertainments.

Since it is essentially accessible only by boat, just getting there is entertainment in itself. A round trip ticket, at less than $10, must surely qualify as one of the best travel bargains anywhere. One may even be assured that more than one shipboard romance has blossomed on that twenty-minute trip.

For boat owners, the waters around Fire Island are an incomparable resource. From jet-skis to classic sailcraft to sumptuous floating palaces, vessels of every description are found in abundance.

Fishing is fabulous. Charter boats are available for ocean and bay fishing, surfcasting is enjoyed, bayside docks are well used. One can catch Blue-Claw crabs with a net and a fishhead, or dig succulent hard clams with the feet.

Sports? Surfing, sailboarding, scuba diving, snorkeling and water-skiing are popular. Many communities have volleyball nets, tennis and basketball courts, athletic fields for organized softball games or impromptu soccer matches. Some hold organized footraces. Ocean Beach has a municipal swimming pool; Robert Moses State Park has a pitch-putt golf course. Duck hunting is permitted seasonally in Wilderness areas.

Many communities host plays, concerts, art shows, picnics and parades. There's a movie theater at Ocean Beach, and even an aerobics studio. Fine restaurants and places to dance may be found all over the Island.

Fire Island is truly a cornucopia of delights. This book offers a sampling of its scenes and seasons and souvenirs. Enjoy!

FIRE ISLAND INLET

Fire Island Inlet feeds and drains the Great South Bay and also forms the western end of Fire Island. Its fast tides and white sands are familiar to countless fishermen and boaters.

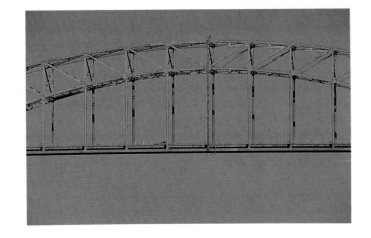

Above: Robert Moses Bridge is part of the Robert Moses Causeway, western gateway to Fire Island.

Below: Fire Island looking west from Robert Moses State Park to Fire Island Inlet

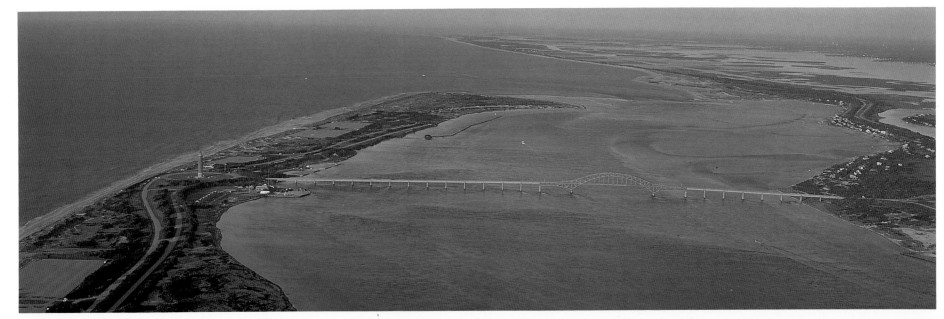

R.M.S.P. WATER TOWER

Left, below and far left: Robert Moses State Park Water Tower

Left, above: Seen west of Fire Island Light is Ivan Kadar in his home-built kayak. It features a foot-operated rudder of his own design that facilitates the craft's use in the Ocean.

Right and above: Fire Island Light, Fire Island's most famous landmark operated from 1858 until 1974, when it was replaced with a beacon on the R.M.S.P. water tower. Popular demand, private fundraising and Park Service muscle relit it in 1986.

ROBERT MOSES STATE PARK

Robert Moses State Park is, by far, Fire Island's largest public facility, with parking for 8300 cars.

These and all subsequent aerial photos by Bill Rudock / Our View Photography

The Kismet Zoo

Kismet has sun, surf, sand and suds but no one'll ever ask you for your pedigree papers.

Kismet Harbor

Basketball at Kismet

The Kismet Inn

The Kismet Out

12

From the Air

Sentinels

The Public Dock

SALTAIRE

Clam Pond Cove, Fire Island's only natural harbor.

Above: Clam Pond Marsh, with "Our Lady by the Sea" R.C. Church in the background.

Saltaire is one of Fire Island's most distinctive communities. It's well-bred and elegant, but casual and friendly.

A Meeting of the Saltaire Citizen's Advisory Association

Town Dock

Zoë Aloft

Best Friend

Bay Beach 17

Saltaire

Fair Harbor

The "Sixish," Fair Harbor's highest-profile institution, is alive and well; as multitudes gather on the public dock to toast the setting of the weekend sun.

Dunewood, Fire Island's newest community, was built as a single tract in 1958.

Right: Dunewood Yacht Club's Sunfish Armada

Port Of Entry

Boats at Anchor

LONELYVILLE

This Page: Lonelyville is one of Fire Island's older communities. The house at left and upper left is nick-named "The Shack" and was built from two Sears garage kits back to back. That at top center was built over the old donkey barn from Capt. Selah Clock's original fishing operation of the 1880's. At upper right is a newer model from newer East Lonelyville.

Right Page: Scenes from Atlantique; both the original hamlet and the neighboring Islip Town Marina, built in 1962.

ROBBIN'S REST

A regular sight at pocket-sized Robbin's Rest is that of thoroughbred race horses training in the Bay to build muscle.

Friends

The Club

A private community just west of Ocean Beach, Fire Island Summer Club uses the former U.S. Coast Guard station from Blue Point as a clubhouse.

CORNEILLE ESTATES

Dana Wallace, "Town Squire"

Kata

Once part of Ocean Beach, now private, Corneille Estates houses Fire Island's only school, which operates year-round.

Dunewood

Lonelyville

Atlantique

Robbin's Rest

Fire Island Summer ___ / Corneille Estates

31

Ferry Terminal at Bay Shore

Boatride to Freedom

The Late Public Phones

The Fire Island Family Car

Ocean Beach is Fire Island's Metropolis. It incorporated in 1921 and has <u>everything</u>. Some live here all year.

The Grill

Art Fair

A Den of Authority

Out to Lunch

Pistils n' Peat

Street Scene

The Seaview market offers dockside shopping.

Seaview is prosperous, comfortable, quiet and classy. Its homes are varied and handsome.

Titus and Bicycles

Annual Association Picnic

Seaview

Ocean Bay Park

Ocean Bay Park is a creation of the Flynn Dynasty. It's known for its freedom, youthfulness and fun.

Above and Left: Flynn's Restaurant dates to 1937 and has since been one of Fire Island's most popular dinner destinations.

The Hotel

The Motel

Firetrucks

Boat People

POINT O' WOODS

Private spacious, conservative, decidedly upscale Point O' Woods is little known to other Islanders. It's lovely.

Shrinking Strand

A Canopied Walk

P.O.W.'s Unique Railway

Sailing Instruction

Left: The Club   Point O' Woods

OAKLEYVILLE

The Road Rarely Taken

Guardian of the Gate

Family Home for 70 Years

With no public anything, tiny Oakleyville defines obscure on Fire Island. It's not even on most maps.

SAILOR'S HAVEN / SUNKEN FOREST

This National Park Service site offers interpretive activities, walks through the magnificent Sunken Forest, extensive public facilities, lifeguarded beaches.

The lower photos show the early Coast Guard's lifesaving drill. (F.I.N.S. Photo)

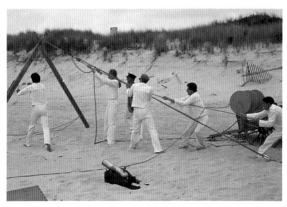

CHERRY GROVE

Christie

Cherry Grove Beach Club

Left: Pool

Right: Bar

Fire Island's most famous community, Cherry Grove is Gay, flamboyant and fun. Alive around the clock, its freedom is unmatched anywhere.

Right:
Michael's Restaurant

Far Right: Disco

The "Belvedere" Guest House

At Night

FIRE ISLAND PINES

Fire Island Pines is the Island's glamour capital. Wooded walks, swimming pools, gorgeous homes, gorgeous people.

Seaflower

Pines Boardwalk

Deck at the Boatel

Magic Carpet Ride

A Rainy Day

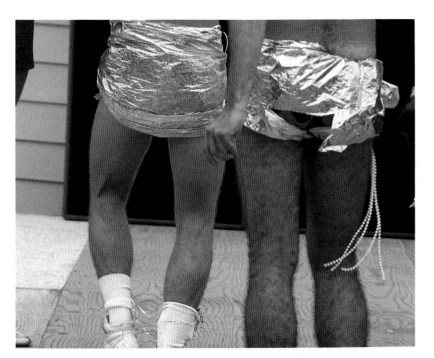

Gay Men's Health Crisis Morning Party, A Benefit for AIDS

Smoky Hollow Bog, at the west end of the Pines, exhibits the most amazing colors. It was
one of the earliest properties in New York State deeded to the Nature Conservancy.

Barrett Beach, above and right, is an Islip Town Beach frequented by Long Island families, teenagers and boatowners.

Talisman, once a private resort, then FINS headquarters for a time, offers beach access and picnic facilities. Also, the Seashore maintains a lab for the use of various scientific researchers. At center, below, Dr. Howard Ginsberg conducts a study on Deer Ticks.

WATER ISLAND

Without electricity until 1974, Water Island has only recently begun to relinquish
its rusticity with the construction of a number of Pines-like palaces.

Lazy Day

Downtown Water Island

BLUE POINT BEACH

Blue Point Beach has only twelve homes. You don't get there easily.
Its residents wouldn't leave easily, either.

A Fire Island newcomer, Davis Park is a mainstream, middle-class neighborhood with few pretensions. It is the destination of choice for Brookhaven Town boatowners.

Good Chicken

This Table's Taken

Bay View

Dancing at the Casino

Davis Park

Good Afternoon

The Annual Independence Day Parade

A Typical Harbor Weekend

Watch Hill is another Fire Island National Seashore facility. Shown here are the marina and nature walk.

Bridge, Nature Trail

Marina

Burma Road

Family Campsites

Goldenrod

Glasswort

Cattails

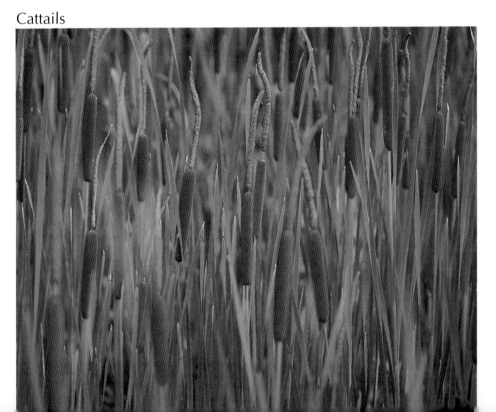

A Bog

LONG COVE

Long Cove is a tiny "squatter's community" east of Watch Hill. It is living on borrowed time, as inholders' leases expire in 1993.

Bellport Beach, run by the town of Bellport, is served by a small ferry that departs when full.

Whalehouse Point was the site of a U.S. Life-saving Service station built in the 1880's.

Old Inlet once had an inlet, but it closed up around the remains of the wrecked Savannah, the first steamship to cross the Atlantic.

Left: One Bellport Beach-goer brought a commitment to sculpt.

Far left: Bellport Beach Boardwalk.

Left: Remains of the old Coast Guard tower at Whalehouse Point.

At right; an unbearably rustic house on Pelican Island, near Old Inlet. The <u>only one</u>.

Parking for <u>Multitudes</u>

The Drawbridge to Mastic

4WD Heaven

Fire Island's Only R.V. Park

Morning Fisherman

Smith Point has a large Suffolk County park, a F.I.N.S. visitor's center, and the East End's only motor vehicle access to the Island.

GREAT GUN BEACH

At Great Gun Beach, east of Smith Point, eastbound 4WD traffic is diverted inland to the Burma Road. There's a public dock here for Moriches beachgoers.

After a storm breached the Barrier Beach in 1931, it was found that the Bay benefitted from the increased water flow. Stabilizing the Inlet has been problematic ever since. Inset: Storm Damage, 1980 (F.I.N.S. Photo)

HOMES

Left to right, top to bottom: 1) Coffey House, Saltaire 2) Fair Harbor 3) Corneille Estates 4) Seaview 5) "Shells", Ocean Beach 6) Robbin's Rest 7) Atlantique 8) Seaview

Left to right, top to bottom: 1) Cherry Grove 2- 5) Fire Island Pines (2 shows "The Co-ops", the only condominiums on Fire Island, dating to 1960.) 6,7) Water Island 8,9) Davis Park

"THE ARK"

"The Ark," in Ocean Beach, is one of Fire Island 's most historic houses. Said to have been built as the "Olympic Club House" in Islip, it was floated to the Island in 1905, later became a well-known guest house. It is currently owned by travel publishers Bert and Luisita Lief.

Photo by L. Lief

Left: Our Lady of the Magnificat, Ocean Beach

Right: Fire Island Synagogue, Seaview

Left: The Church at Point O'Woods

Right: Union Free Protestant Church, Ocean Beach

BEHIND THE SCENES

Top to Bottom, Left to Right: 1) Tony's Sanitation Barge, Fire Island Pines 2) Electrician, Ocean Beach 3) Freight Boat, F.I.P. 4) Roofer, Fair Harbor 5) Carpenters, F.I.P. 6) Carpenter's Flatbed, F.I.P. 7) Freight Boat, Fair Harbor 8) Fire Dept., Ocean Beach 9) Painter, Seaview

L.I.L.C.O. Electric Substation, Fire Island Pines

Municipal Water Supply, Seaview

Bottled Gas, F.I.P.

Sewage Treatment Facility, Ocean Beach

DANGER
WALK
CLOSED

FLORA

Shadblow

Beachgrass

Pitch Pine (F.I.N.S. Photo)

Poison Ivy

Phragmites

Bearberry

Beach Plum (F.I.N.S. Photo)

Salt Spray Rose (F.I.N.S.)

Catbrier

FAUNA

Fowler's Toad

Grey Squirrel

Praying Mantis with Monarch

Buckeye

Red Fox (F.I.N.S. Photo)

Cottontail Rabbit

Snapping Turtle

Meadow Vole

Black Racer (F.I.N.S.)

Norway Rat

DEER

Deer are everywhere on Fire Island. They interact with people and pets. As their numbers increase, and because they host a tick that carries Lyme Disease, they generate controversy. But they are unquestionably magnificent.

During the course of compiling this book, I ran across Warren Wexler at Cherry Grove. He is one of the few hardy, sovereign souls that stay all year at Fire Island; and he passes many solitary days exploring and experiencing a wonderland that most of us will never see. He seems an uncommonly contented man and appears to, well, know things that many of us may not. He told me of an encounter he'd had on one of those days:

A few weeks back, while walking through the Sunken Forest, I saw two stags lying down. I began softly chanting a low tone and very slowly walked towards them.

As I came near, one of them quickly rose and moved off some twenty feet. I stopped. The bigger stag also rose, but slowly, looking at me all the while, then took a few steps towards me. I saw how big his approaching antlers were. Five feet from me, as I continued to chant, he stopped and sniffed my scent. Then he lowered his head to graze on the low green ground cover. We stood like that awhile, five feet apart, me chanting, him grazing.

He raised his head, again sniffed the air between us, then slowly walked past me. The smaller stag fell in behind him, and I followed, some eight feet behind the second stag, keeping to their pace.

The three of us walked leisurely through the forest, single-file, me toning all the while, them pausing occasionally to graze. I didn't know anymore where in the forest I was.

The big stag moved to the top of a rise and then laid down in a clearing. The second stag went to the nearest knoll and also laid down. I walked up the rise and sat down on the earth eight feet from the big stag. I continued softly chanting, and gradually moved closer, until we were lying side by side. We stayed like that for a while, calmly, not moving, just being there.

The stag rose, stretching his legs, grazed a bit, and then started moving off. The second stag again fell in behind, and so did I, the three of us resuming our walk through the forest. After we had gone a ways, the two of them paused to graze and I sat down on top of a

small dune a few feet off. The big stag moved towards me, grazing as he approached. He came to within two feet, then laid down alongside me.

Again, we stayed like that awhile, neither of us moving very much, while the second stag continued grazing near us.

I remembered that I had my little 35 - millimeter camera with me, took it out, and, over the next few minutes, snapped some close-ups. The stag remained serene.

Finally, the big stag rose, once again sniffed the air between us, then joined the other. I sat there watching the two of them slowly moving off through the trees into the distance.

After a few more seconds, I stood, turned, and walked slowly back to find the trail.

- Warren Boyd Wexler -

Photos This Page by Warren Wexler

A GALLERY OF BOATS

Top to Bottom, Left to Right: 1) Cutter 2) Hobie Cat 3) Jet Ski 4) Sportfisherman 5) "Crazy Charlie" 6) High Performance Runabout 7) Sloop 8) Motor Yacht 9) Clammer and Friend

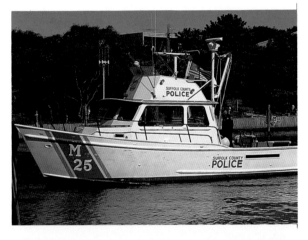

Top to Bottom, Left to Right: 1) Freight Boat, Cherry Grove 2) U.S. Coast Guard Rescue Boat 3) Gaff-Rigged "Catboat" 4) Suffolk County Police Dept. Patrol Boat 5) Sunlit Helm 6) Modern Viking, Davis Park 7) Iceboats 8) Inflatable

109

FERRIES

Left: For most the only Fire Island access, ferries are a necessary good. On them, the adventure begins, the week's worries recede.

This page: Several companies offer water taxi service between Fire Island communities; an alternative to enforced isolation. How lucky for us.

FOG

SPORTS

Basketball at Ocean Beach

Pitch-Putt Golf at Robert Moses S.P.

Softball at Saltaire

Volleyball at Seaview

Tennis Lessons at Fire Island Summer Club

Touch Football at Saltaire

Duck Hunting, National Wilderness

Ted Lap Photo

"Surf City" is an area east of Smith Point known for its consistently good waves. These pictures were taken after the passage of the tail of a tropical storm.

Left: Boogie Boarder at Fire Island Pines on the same weekend.

117

MISS FIRE ISLAND CONTEST

This notorious "Drag Queen" pageant is one of the social highlights of the season at Cherry Grove. Small wonder.

NATURAL LIFE ZONES

Salt Marsh/ Mud Flat

Freshwater Bog

Bog/ Marine Forest

Marine Forest

Pine Forest

Thicket/ Swale

Swale/ Secondary Dune

Primary Dune

The Annual Davis Park Sailboat Shootout

BIRDS

Top to Bottom, Left to Right: 1) Cape May Warbler 2) Swans 3) Black-Backed Gull 4) Common Terns 5) Saw-Whet Owl (F.I.N.S. Photo)
6) Catbird 7) Brown Thrasher 8) Oyster Catchers (F.I.N.S.) 9) Canada Geese

Cormorants (Ted Lap Photo)

Seagulls

Sanderlings

Mallard

Great Egret

FISHING

Fishing, not surprisingly on an island in fertile waters, is a popular pastime and takes many forms. Still, this picture depicts an unusual enterprise. It is not altered in any way, just a product of luck.

A Bayfishing Charter Boat from Bay Shore

The Ones That Didn't Get Away

An Ocean Boat from Captree

Surfcasting

TEXTURES

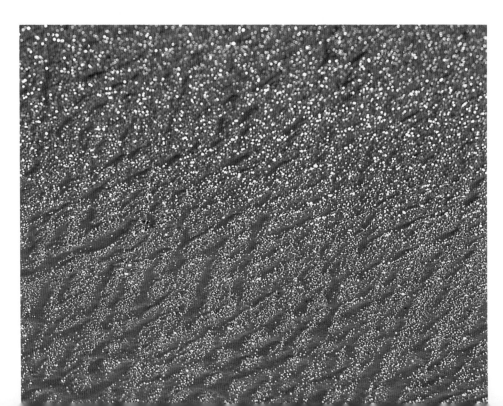

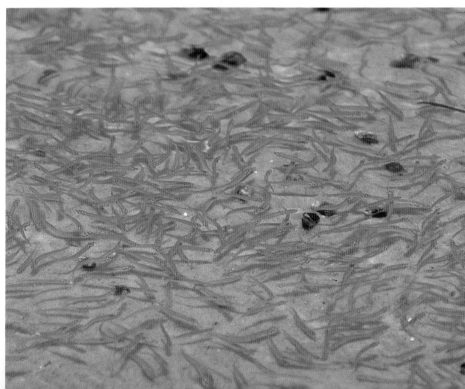

BEACHCOMBING

131

KITE FESTIVAL

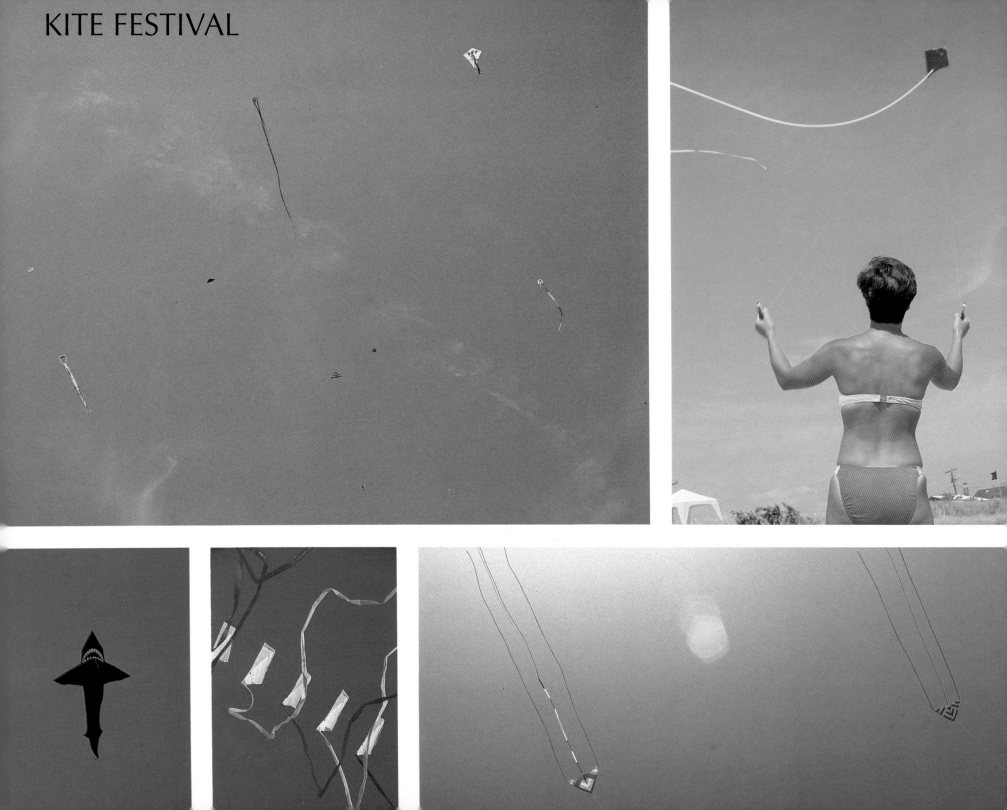

Fair Harbor

Ocean Beach

Seaview

Fire Island Pines

Fire Island Pines

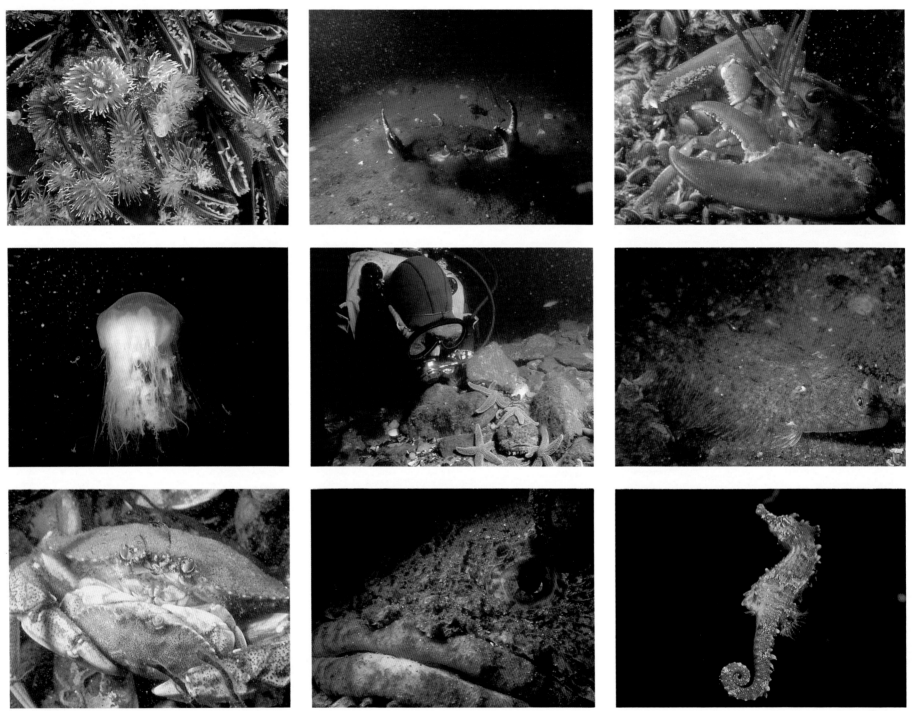

Top to Bottom, Left to Right: 1) Mussels and Anemones 2) Calico Crab 3) Lobster 4) "Lion's Mane" Jellyfish 5) Starfish 6) Flounder
7) Rock Crabs Mating 8) Toadfish 9) Sea Horse

Left: The waters around Fire Island teem with marine life. These extraordinary pictures by Pete Nawrocky show creatures typical of the Great South Bay. All you need are a mask and a snorkel to gain admittance to this marvelous world often only inches below the surface....

This page: The area of the Atlantic Ocean that includes Long Island's South Shore and the New Jersey Coast is known as the New York Bight, or, more colloquially, "Wreck Valley." There are numerous shipwrecks here, more than ninety of which are documented in Dan Berg's excellent book by the same name, One of the most famous off of Fire Island is the "San Diego," a cruiser that was the only major warship lost by the U.S. during World War I. She was probably the victim of a German mine.

All Photos by Pete Nawrocky.

The "San Diego" keelside up in 90 feet of water

Small Arms Locker

Brass Cage Lantern

Boiler Room 135

FALL

Saltaire

Maple Leaves

Fair Harbor

Happiness Isn't....

Virginia Creeper

Pines Boatel

Maple Tree, Ocean Beach

Seaview Playground

Fence, Kismet

This is November, honest!

Saltaire

No Crowds to Fight

Casino, Davis Park

Getting Short

Fire Island Pines

Winter Walk

All *Winter* photos courtesy Fire Island National Seashore except as noted.

"Scooter"

Bay Ice

Ice Floes on Bayshore

Sailskating

Baywater Freezing

Snowcovered Beach

Bayard C. Fenner Photo   Pines Harbor

Smith Point After Blizzard

Shadblow in Snow 143

SUNSET